Praise for
Breaking Your Loyalty Contract

"*Breaking Your Loyalty Contract* is a must read for everyone. Through generational and environmental conditioning, we inherit the best and not-so-best traits from our parents. By the time we're in grade school, the groundwork has been laid and our paradigm is set. If a child is raised with praise, that child will grow up to be a confident adult. Conversely, if a child is raised in an environment where "no" is often heard, the child quickly adapts and stops asking questions and will quite often adapt an attitude of "no". Children should be encouraged to take risks, to think for themselves, to make mistakes, and to learn and to grow from their mistakes. *Breaking Your Loyalty Contract* is the perfect guide for every parent to read through to better understand their children and themselves."

— **Bob Proctor,**
Teacher in The Secret and best-selling
author of You Were Born Rich

"Maria has brilliantly shared her own wisdom, experience and understanding in a way that can truly save you years of time and help prevent you from going down a challenging road.

If you are looking for guidance that can help transform your life in a positive way, look no further than the pages of this wonderful book."

— Peggy McColl
New York Times Best Selling
Author http://PeggyMcColl.com

"In working with Maria, I experienced her as a gifted therapist with an eye for the essential. She is empathetic and helps clients successfully on their way. She is flexible and able to take unusual paths."

— Sabine Lück
Psychological Psychotherapist,
Instructor, Author

"I know Maria because we have a common interest. The enormous and life-determining influence of childhood on the social climate in our society concerns us both. We need more attention in our society for the conditions in which children grow up. Maria is deeply committed and has a special way of bringing people to the source of their relationships and feelings. I wish her the best to bring a paradigm shift to our society."

—Jay Belsky
Professor of Human Development,
University of California, Davis
Child Psychologist, Author

"I have perceived Maria as an honest, sincere and inspiring personality. With her optimistic attitude, she has been committed to paying more attention to the vulnerability of early childhood and to the connection between childhood and quality of life in old age for decades."

— **Rüdiger Rogoll**
Psychiatrist, Psychotherapist, Author

"Maria is a family-oriented and sincere pediatrician and family therapist who dedicates herself to the real needs of children with much effort and boldness."

— **Steve Biddulph**
Author and Psychologist

Breaking
YOUR
LOYALTY
Contract

Shattering the Mirror Effect
Between Parents and Children

by

MARIA STEUER

Hasmark
PUBLISHING
INTERNATIONAL

Editor:
Kathryn Young
kathryn@hasmarkpublishing.com

Cover & Book Design:
Anne Karklins
anne@hasmarkpublishing.com

ISBN 13: 978-1-989756-41-6
ISBN 10: 1989756417

Dedication

This book is dedicated to Niklas, Jonas, and Theresa, who have chosen me as their mother to accompany them in their lives.

Acknowledgements

I thank all who supported me and never stopped believing in me.

Table of Contents

Introduction

Can disloyalty pave the path to joyful parenting? Yes, it can. This book tells you why.

Contracts and Limits

You love your children, and you would do anything for them. The bond you have with them includes an unspoken loyalty contract through which you pledge to love them, nourish them, and protect them.

Your children also have a silent loyalty agreement by which they pledge to follow the rules, be faithful to your family, and exhibit behaviors that align with your expectations.

If only the trials and tribulations of parenting were this simple – but they are not!

What makes parenting a challenge is that your children are the only ones who can push you to or beyond your limits.

If your boss pushes you to your limits, you can quit your job. If you are in a relationship with a partner who pushes you past your limits – you can leave the relationship.

However, your children are your children for life. And when their behavior stretches you to your limits, you have no choice but to face the challenge and find a solution.

The Answers You Seek Can Be Found In Your Past

In this book, I invite you to explore why issues from your *own* childhood are being reflected back to you through your child's misbehavior, like a mirror effect.

For example, as a child, you may have been discouraged from being a free thinker who developed your own ideas about how you wanted to live.

As a result, the unspoken loyalty contract you have with your parents may have motivated you to suppress your free-thinking instincts and form a belief that "thinking outside the lines" of your parents' expectations was bad behavior.

As a parent, you may now recognize free-thinking characteristics in your child and view them as bad behavior due to the subconscious loyalty contract you still have with your parents.

Set Yourself Free

Breaking Your Loyalty Contract provides you with a set of mental tools and exercises you need to break the subconscious agreements you have with your parents.

The decision to break these agreements empowers you to take back aspects of your personality you surrendered to your parents as a child.

Doing this liberates you to be your true self and to view your children through a prism of who *they* are, instead of seeing them through the prism of what your parents expected *you* to be.

By exploring your childhood and understanding why you think the way you think, you will gain the clarity you need to:

Understand what is in your subconscious blind spots as a parent (*we all have them!*)

Ask self-questions that dissolve buried belief systems that have impeded your growth

Recognize that what you view as faults in your children may actually be gifts

Release your children and yourself from unreasonable expectations so you both can thrive and flourish

You will also gain a clear understanding that behavior exhibited by your child need not be labeled as bad simply because your parents labeled it as such when they saw it in you.

Concise and to the Point

I have structured *Breaking Your Loyalty Contract* so that its chapters are brief, to the point, and concise. In fact, the entire book can be read in a single sitting.

This brevity allows you to absorb and understand the probing lessons and tools I share more easily.

The compact format of *Breaking Your Loyalty Contract* also makes it simple to revisit and review chapters and sections that resonate with you most.

Know Your *Why* and the *How* Will Follow

The beauty of *Breaking Your Loyalty Contract* is that I have not written a recipe book that tells you what to do and how, so this is no how-to parenting book.

How-to books usually offer cookie-cutter parenting solutions that tempt you to compare your results to those that can be achieved "according to the book."

This approach can cause you to judge yourself too harshly and sway you to believe you are not a good parent when, in fact, you are.

Instead, with *Breaking Your Loyalty Contract*, I encourage you to explore your childhood to discover *why* you think the way you think. The moment you understand your *why*, your *how-to* method will flow into your heart and be uniquely your own.

Emotional Nourishment Is Vital

When you learn to release loyalty contracts with your parents that have tied you to limiting belief systems, you will be able to revitalize your relationships with your children.

As essential as nourishment, protection, and shelter are, what your kids really crave is a close emotional relationship with you that makes them feel loved unconditionally.

This feeling is what sets the stage for a healthy frame of mind that can last them a lifetime.

Breaking Your Loyalty Contract is like a permission slip to explore your childhood and your family dynamic. The journey you undertake will be inspiring and transformative.

After you read this book, you will feel empowered in your ability to step away from generational regulations, well-intentioned advice, and family constraints.

When you do, you will be free to make parenting your children the joyous journey it is meant to be.

I also promise you that, without you realizing it, your relationships with yourself, your partner, your boss, and other friends will also change!

Maria Steuer
mariasteuer.com

Chapter One

Courage to Face Facts

Let the past make you better, not bitter.

— **Buddhist quote**

How often in my professional life have I heard the statement, "If I had known that I would have done it differently!" It has happened so often that I cannot count how many times.

I have written this book so that this situation does not have to happen to you. You do not have to learn something only to find it is too late to use what you've learned. You do not want to discover that you missed something important. However, had you known in time; would you have made a different decision? Or is this simply an empty phrase you use in frustration because it is already too late to change your course?

People are creatures of habit. They naturally resist change. Change is uncomfortable, annoying, and unsettling, so all too often, we employ ignorance as a simple solution. Because we do not like to deal with situations that mandate change, we try simply to ignore such things. Even more easily, we might blame the circumstances.

Imagine yourself in the following scenario. You have a partner who always treats you badly, and you do not feel comfortable in the relationship. You would like to have a great partnership, and a change would be needed to accomplish this. However, initiating such a change, and its uncertain outcome, is uncomfortable at first. Due to the uncertainty and discomfort, you ignore the problems and talk yourself into staying in the relationship, telling yourself that it could be worse; or you blame the circumstances. *My partner has tremendous stress at work*, you think, *and he can't help it.* Either way, you come to believe that change is not necessary.

Few situations in life put us in the awkward position of striving for personal change. One of these few situations is the behaviour of our children. Children have a special ability, through their behaviour, to hold a mirror up to us. A child cannot simply be ignored or reduced to background noise. Children literally force us into change because they do not easily control their behaviour. A boisterous, energetic, talkative child can be difficult to deal with if the child accompanies you in social situations and, for example, inappropriately interrupts adult conversation. You try to correct the situation, but no matter what you try, nothing changes. Perhaps you blame the circumstances, and in the future, either decline invitations to social situations or find a way to leave your child at home.

But the best solution might start by looking for the root causes of undesirable behaviour. Could the child's behaviour have something to do with you, what you are doing, how you interact with the child? Perhaps you unconsciously reinforce the behaviour of your child with your own behaviour. Look at these connections fearlessly and reflect on them because that's how positive change becomes possible. And do not worry: all parents get to this point!

Parents should develop the courage to see children and their behaviour as a personal opportunity to change a situation for the better. Perhaps parents can be grateful that their children remind them daily that change is necessary and then explore the causes of their children's behaviour, as well as their own.

You can gain knowledge about yourself and come to insights that will bring you to a better life path. These insights would benefit both your children and you because when parents reflect on their own childhood, they can decide consciously how they want to deal with the demands of their children.

If you are parents-to-be, congratulations! All parents have ideas and wishes about how their baby should be and would give everything to make sure their baby does well. They have probably also watched the offspring of friends and, in doing so, quietly discovered the qualities they find great in children. Even before a child's birth, it is worthwhile for parents to explore their own childhood to remember what they considered as good or less good for themselves at that time.

If you have no children, or not yet, what can you get from reading on in this book? You can proactively set out to strive for positive changes. Fearlessly looking at the connections from your childhood can also help you to achieve a better quality of life for yourself. Perhaps such reflection can lead you to finally establish a fulfilling partnership with real closeness.

This book wants to make clear in a short and concise way how we acquired our habits and why we are rarely willing to change habits or replace them with new ones. If we become aware of our impulses for action, we can find sustainable solutions and changes for ourselves and our relationships. Relationships are the focus of this book.

Time is an increasingly scarce resource in today's fast-paced world. Reading is important, but it is much more important that you take time for yourself. I have tried to extract the essentials from a wide variety of theories and approaches and put them into an easily digestible format. To make the book easier to understand, I have only touched upon some aspects. The selection of what approaches and theories to focus on is, of course, personal and reflects in short form my years of professional and personal experience with the topic. I hope I have succeeded, and you manage to read the whole book! Its brevity should encourage you even to read the book several times.

Conclusion

Through my practical work, my personal experiences, and my professional life, I have observed that the most diverse theories that look for explanations for human actions can be reduced to one common statement:

Whether a person finds himself valuable in his life is decided in early childhood, and this can be influenced!

It's easy — but it's not simple.

Chapter Two

Why Not Just Do It Differently?

When it hurts, observe. Life is trying to
teach you something.

— Author unknown

Childhood shapes your life. I think everyone can agree with that statement. How, in what form, and to what extent it does so, however, is not clear to anyone.

Let us look at some examples.

An adult young man of normal weight and proportions tells us that he has a "crazy" problem. When he is in a bad mood, he cannot distinguish between being hungry or having an interpersonal problem, such as being annoyed with someone. He has noticed that when he eats something, the bad mood can suddenly disappear. By chance, he had told his mother about it, and she remembered that when he was a baby, she had not treated him according to all his needs. A midwife had advised her thirty years ago that a nursing child should only be fed every four hours. Therefore, if her son was hungry after only three hours, the mother did not feed him, but carried him around and tried to keep him happy during the hour until feeding time.

A bad mood is an unpleasant feeling, and the same feeling can have different causes. Feelings are emotional memories. This is probably where the inability to distinguish the causes of a bad mood comes from (such as the ability to differentiate between hunger and personal problems). Since the young man now has an explanation for his problem, he always has something to eat in his pocket and does his bad mood test. If he feels better after the snack, it was hunger; otherwise, he has to turn his attention to face other problem solutions.

If the mother had trusted her feelings rather than following the midwife's recommendations and acted accordingly, she would have breastfed her baby immediately. She could have chosen not to put her baby off.

See how far into adulthood a mother's reaction can reach? She had responded to the expression of discomfort, but she did not react properly to the cause (hunger) by providing food. Instead, she responded by comforting, carrying, and calming her baby. Even as an adult, the son, although now aware of the reasons, is not able to distinguish between the two possible causes. He has found a way to deal with this circumstance in a relaxed way. With trial and error, in his case, he can determine the difference.

Here is another example. A mother is in dialogue with her baby. The two make grimaces at each other. The mom tickles her baby and does whatever else comes to her mind. But now, in the middle of this exciting interaction, the mother gets a message on her mobile phone. She interrupts the dialogue with her baby and answers her smartphone; her attention is diverted from her baby. The baby is irritated at first and then tries to get mom's attention back to encourage the mother to continue with their interaction. If this attempt to reconnect does not succeed, the baby becomes sad, turns away, and maybe even starts crying. The baby has just experienced that *a smartphone is more important than itself.*

But other scenarios are also conceivable.

If the baby gets attention and care again when it cries, when the mother puts the smartphone away because of the crying, the baby maybe has learned that *whoever cries gets attention.*

If the baby experiences an angry mother due to its crying, a mother who is annoyed because she had to interrupt her digital communication, then the baby maybe has learned *crying causes trouble.*

So, a baby can experience one situation, but at least three or more different experiences can be stored as feelings.

To understand the context of the situation, you must understand why the baby can react so differently. The baby is very sensitive and immediately senses when the mother is physically present but mentally elsewhere. Stimuli lurk everywhere to distract our attention. But not every distraction is disturbing for the baby! The neighbour ringing the doorbell may distract the mother, but she remains present in her mind by picking up her baby and looking for the cause of the disturbance together. The baby is involved in the process.

Life Plan Created During Childhood

Experts attach special importance to childhood because a life plan is created there in the subconscious. Transactional analysis, as developed by Eric Berne in the late 1950s, calls this life plan a *script.* This life plan is like a tattoo, a stamp that is imprinted on us and shapes us for our lifetime. The script is the reason why a person follows certain patterns of behaviour again and again throughout his life. Humans acquire this script in early childhood through experiences in their environment.

For example, if a child is sent to his room as punishment when he expresses his anger loudly, he may develop the view that *It is not OK to be angry* or *I am not lovable when I am angry*. The child feels unloved, helpless, lonely, and alone. The child stores this experience and wants to avoid the repetition of the bad experience in the future.

As a consequence, in adulthood, the person tries to avoid situations that threaten to become unpleasant. Adults who learned as a child that *I am not lovable when I am angry* develop patterns of behaviour that avoid such experiences. As adults, they can be particularly peaceful and always look for balance. They suppress their anger whenever possible, even when it is inappropriate to suppress it. Instead of banging on the table when their legitimate interests are disregarded, they withdraw because *they cannot get out of their skin*. This has nothing to do with their skin or their character, but rather it is the subconscious life script, developed in early childhood, which prescribes these behaviours.

It would have been better to avoid such a punishment. Instead, it would have made more sense for the parent to reflect with the angry child and to provide brief, nonconfrontational feedback such as, "I see that you are quite angry! What are you angry about, and why are you screaming like that?" The mother could then find a way out of the anger with her child, and at the same time, correct the overreaction without affecting the child as a whole emotionally.

Everything that we experience or miss in the first years of life becomes part of our life plan. All babies have an innate desire for closeness, warmth, and security. Their hunger for attention is great. Only when they manage to capture the attention of their caregiver, do they receive the perceptions that are vital for them. This perception fulfills the longed-for and urgently needed feeling of closeness, warmth, and security. In the first weeks, months, and years, how a person will act and react in later life is shaped; for example, attracting attention and gaining recognition in their professional and private life.

Unfortunately, the reverse is also true: if a small child only gets attention when it shows misbehaviour, such as attention in the form of scolding and punishment, the child will show the behaviour over and over again. Negative attention is still better than no attention at all.

The behaviour that a baby has to display to get the desired attention from the mother or another caregiver is subconsciously imprinted on the baby so that it will act with the same behaviour as an adult.

Early in life, the child begins to internalize which values are exercised and expressed in the family. It learns which role it can best use to cope in this value system. Thus, the child writes its own personal role book. The reason is simple: if the child did not fit into the given value system of the family, it would receive less attention.

Both love and attention are the emotional sustenance for all babies and toddlers, as important as a mother's milk for the infant. This is why children do everything they can to live up to this family value system. The sum of all experiences with our feelings and the experiences of early childhood thus form our subconscious life plan.

Let us assume that we have had the following experience: *I am not worthy to be loved for my own sake* and have consequently (subconsciously) made the decision for our life plan that *I will never find a partner who will stay with me.* Although we are not aware of this decision, we make all the important decisions in our lives in such a way that we are in line with our life plan; as a consequence, we ultimately remain without a partner.

The decisions in childhood are based on the need to receive care and love. Closely related to this is the fear of losing affection if we behave differently. This fear remains with us in adulthood and makes it almost impossible for us to deviate from our early subconscious decisions. As adults, we still believe deep inside that if we act differently than we have learned to act, we will lose the love of our parents, and, of course, we understand that would be a great misfortune for us. Fatally, the subconscious fulfillment of our life plan is of such fundamental importance to us that we are even willing to reinterpret and misjudge reality and adapt it to our life plan. *We adapt reality to the life plan and not the life plan to reality.* Even if there were a partner willing to stay with us, we would push them away to fulfil our life script *because I am not worthy of a partnership.* This process initially is not consciously understood by the person concerned.

A small child does not question parental commands, rules, and principles. It cannot evaluate these guidelines because its thinking skills have not yet fully developed. Rather, the infant looks for clues to ways to please its parents, or to at least gain their attention.

With this behaviour, we encounter yet another dilemma. We wish that the world would be as we experienced it as a small child, and as our parents explained the world to us. If we see and experience consciously that this is not the case, then our parents would have been wrong, and we do not want to consider that.

At the age of seven, our life plan is mostly finished. We now believe we know how the world works, how it reacts to us, and how we should deal with it. We continue to work on it as young people and revise one aspect or the other, but the older a person gets, the less they change.

As an example of a change, a mother experienced rejection and emotional coldness in her own childhood. Nevertheless, as a mother, she is extremely loving, patient, and empathetic with her four small children. She tells us that as a schoolchild, she had a friend with a very loving mother whom she often visited. She felt she was seen and liked there and decided that if she ever had children, she would become a mother like the one her friend had. She had been given a chance, which she took and decided to take a different path.

So, parents pass on positive and negative messages to their children that should be fulfilled. Positive messages are permissions about the parent's approval regarding the child's behaviour. Permission could be *to ask for what you want*. Negative messages appear when the parents are disapproving of the child's behaviour. Rüdiger Rogoll, one of the most important transactional analysis therapists in the German-speaking world, has summarized eight important basic negative messages. They are not explicitly given but are passed on by the parents through facial expressions, body language, or actions. They are expressions of disappointment, frustration, anxiety, and unhappiness which come out of the parent's own pain. Both sides, parents and children, act on a subconscious level. Since we are not aware of these messages, they sound very strange. It is possible that, while reading them, one or more of these messages may touch something in you. It is possible that feelings from your childhood are addressed.

Negative and Positive Messages

The eight injunctions (subconscious negative messages), according to Rogoll, are as follows:

- Do not feel, do not show any feelings
- Do not be a child, grow up
- Do not be close
- Do not be you
- Do not be well
- Do not think
- Do not feel
- Do not succeed

Why do parents do this? Because they pass on their own unreflected messages from their parents to their children. This way, the same issues can persist in a family for several generations. *Don't be healthy*, for example, arises when a child experiences over the years that they receive special attention and care whenever they are ill. The child has learned to become ill and, in this way, to get attention from the caregiver. Even as adults, they try to get attention for themselves by being sick.

Parents, however, also give their children positive advice in the form of commandments for their life path. And, like the subconscious negative messages, parents often pass their own advice from their parents to their children. They react to the difficulties they have with the children.

Transactional analysis has defined five drivers (positive advice):

- Be perfect
- Please others / Please me
- Try hard
- Be strong
- Hurry up

If a child receives (subconsciously) the message *Do not succeed* from its parents, then the child will rarely finish school with good grades. To help the child, the parents now advise, *Try hard*. For the child, this is now a hopeless situation – checkmate! They were taught *Do not succeed* and get the advice *Try hard*. How is this possible together? The child follows the driver and really tries hard, but the injunction, unfortunately, is more powerful; therefore, the child will not succeed despite all efforts.

Injunctions are subconsciously communicated rather than explicitly named, and they develop as we are babies. Drivers are articulated consciously and only become relevant at a later stage of life. The injunction *Do not be healthy* will certainly not be consciously thought or even pronounced by anyone. Drivers such as *Hurry up* or *Make an effort*, on the other hand, are certainly heard by children.

In the example above, the schoolchild is checkmated by the advice. How and with which advice we as parents react is of importance. The child would be helped if the parents give him the opportunity to experience success in another area. In this way, he could then transfer his positive experiences into his school life. When a child repeatedly experiences certain things, it develops certain views of itself, of other people, and of life.

Four Possible Life Positions

With all these experiences, messages, and advice, four possible life positions develop later on, which result in the basic attitude of a person towards their fellow human beings. The four different basic attitudes would look like this:

I'm OK – You're OK.

I'm OK – You're not OK.

I'm not OK – You're OK.

I'm not OK – You're not OK.

For a better understanding, let us look at an example. Imagine that a participant enters a seminar room where other participants are already sitting. This person, called Sarah, could think according to her basic attitude, the corresponding thought:

Basic Attitude	Thought
I'm OK – You're OK.	*I'm curious about what the group will bring.*
I'm OK – You're not OK.	*There are strange people here.*
I'm not OK – You're OK.	*I'm sure they are all better than me.*
I'm not OK – You're not OK.	*This is going to go badly for all of us.*

How we react to certain situations in later life depends on the basic attitude we adopted or were taught in early childhood.

Many things happen involuntarily in the first decisive years of life. We have little or no conscious influence on our life plan. Only the basic attitude *I'm OK – You're OK,* allows us to build happy and lasting relationships with other persons.

Become Aware of Your Life Plan

As a parent, it makes sense to become aware of your own life plan. Only then can we consciously make our own new decisions. Only then can we avoid passing on our negative injunctions and drivers to our children.

Here is another example to consider.

A couple is standing at the train station and saying goodbye after the weekend together. They want to arrange a new weekend to visit at the man's home. The woman asks him when she should come. He replies, "I don't care."

Now guess the great influence the unconscious life script has based on his reply. For example, if she has the inculcation *Don't care,* she will be hurt because she assumes that he doesn't care if she comes or not. If she has the inculcation *Don't feel* and the driver *Be strong,* she will not show her hurt or her feelings. She will retreat, and he will not understand the reason at first. In addition, if his life script is marked by the inculcation *Do not make it,* he will feel confirmed in his script. He had unconsciously provoked this reaction to confirm his injunction. Perhaps he only wanted to say, "Any time is fine with me. The main thing is that you come around!"

Conclusion

All our later behaviour patterns can be explained by the imprinting in early childhood. We should reflect on these patterns and change them if necessary.

It is important for parents to understand this connection: *my behaviour shapes the behaviour of my child.*

By knowing your life plan, you can change your life. Otherwise, situations will occur again and again in life, which we cannot understand and which we think we cannot influence.

Chapter Three

You Can't Change Anything Anyway

Children are not a distraction from more important work.
They are the most important work.

— Dr. John Trainer

I can't do it!
It's no use!

You can't change anything anyway!

Whoever has such attitudes believes they have no influence on anything in their life. The prevailing feeling in the person is this: *I can't do anything about it anyway. I have no control over my life. The circumstances of life dominate me. I lack the belief that I can change that.*

Those thoughts sound like giving up and resigning.

Why is Self-Efficacy Important?

Self-efficacy is the conviction that one can master even the greatest problems through one's own actions. The inner trust that you can successfully perform an action is a matter of course.

Self-efficacy is of great importance for both private and professional success. Self-efficacy allows a person to actively shape his or her life. Self-efficacy is a prerequisite for *resilience*, the ability to cope with mental crises.

A lack of self-efficacy leads to passivity up to the point of shutting down. *Why should I make an effort if I can't manage it anyway!* The Canadian psychologist Albert Bandura came to the conclusion that in order to start an action at all, people must be convinced that they can actually master it successfully. We only start something if we believe we can do it.

For example, children with little self-efficacy show little or no willingness to make an effort at school. If such a child is faced with a math problem and does not find the solution at the first attempt, the child feels no inner need to at least try. These children give up quickly, and they say, *I can't do it.*

At the present time, there are many offers for children and young people to learn self-efficacy. Parents are trained to help their children become self-effective. Parents are given advice such as *Encourage your child* or *Trust your child.*

Why are we describing this topic here in such detail? Once again, the foundation for self-efficacy in later life is laid in early childhood. The offers of help come too late. It is better to prevent rather than correct later.

According to Albert Bandura, self-efficacy arises and grows from the following factors:

- Control your emotions.
- Make positive experiences.
- Look for role models (imitation).
- Let us encourage you (social support).

Parents should consider the following four factors when handling their baby and toddler:

- Help your child to regulate his or her emotions and develop stress regulators.
- Help your child to have positive experiences by giving him tasks he can handle.
- Be a role model for your children.
- Give your child courage.

Self-efficacy is acquired in early childhood, in which only the subconscious mind is available to the child. Conscious, logical, and strategic thinking is not yet developed. Therefore, parents have the task of intervening with their child's consciousness in a regulatory way.

Regulating Emotions and Stress

Let us look at the first factor in more detail. How can you help your child to regulate his emotions and to deal with stress?

A baby lets its parents know, relatively easily, when it is under stress: it cries! Crying is the baby's expression of stress. They cry to alert the parents that something is wrong. Stress activates the alarm systems in a child's brain. Now parents are the regulators, the rescuers, who help them to regain control of their state of arousal.

A baby is born with about 200 billion brain cells, but these cells are not yet linked to each other. That is why the *primitive* or *emotional* brain sets the tone for the very first time. This brain is not able to do a reality check. It cannot assess situations, whether danger is imminent or not. This assessment must be made by the parents. Infants, therefore, orient themselves according to the assessment of their attachment persons.

If, for example, a dog runs towards a small child without the dog being leashed, the orienting look to mom or dad comes immediately. If the parents are relaxed, the child is relaxed. If the adult reacts with obvious fright and is afraid of the dog, the small child also reacts the same. In this way, the child learns to assess situations more and more. This learning process corresponds to the increasing interconnection of brain cells.

Ninety percent of the growth of the brain, including the formation of nerve tracts and connections, takes place in the first five years of life. The parental style of upbringing determines which nerve tracts are created and connected. The parental style of upbringing, therefore, also determines which nerve pathways are formed and how they are connected to each other. Is the child more likely to develop alarm systems or antianxiety systems? These systems, in turn, decide later on the child's social and emotional intelligence.

Babies cry for a variety of reasons. They are hungry or tired; they feel something as too hard, too loud, too bright, too cold; they are separated from the attachment person. All this is stress for a baby. It is not the crying itself that affects the developing brain of the child, but the long-lasting, uncomforted grief. The screaming, or the switching on of the alarm system, leads to the release of the stress hormone cortisol. If there is no adequate consoling or calming, the cortisol levels remain elevated. The alarm system, without regulatory aid, causes permanently increased cortisol levels. Unfortunately, these permanently elevated cortisol levels lead to damage to nerve cells and nerve tracts in the developmental phase of the brain. This means brain cell death through stress.

If parents do not react to their baby's crying and leave it to its own devices, it will finally cry less. In the situation of prolonged crying, meaning uncomforted distress, the child remains without regulatory help and feels hopeless. This should not be confused with inner calmness. An inner calming has not taken place for the child. The level of stress hormones in such a situation is often even higher than during crying. The price of such an adjustment is programming for physical hyperexcitability and an attitude of life marked by fear. That is why the way parents listen, play, hug, and comfort their child is so important.

You may find it difficult to find out why your baby is crying. Over time, you will be able to tell why it is crying. You will learn to distinguish between hungry and tired whines. There may be times when you cannot tell why your baby is crying. The good news is that in this case, the reason does not matter. What really matters is that you calm your baby down and take their crying seriously.

When parents respond sensitively to their baby, the connections can be formed in the child's brain that will enable them to cope with stress later in life, to enter into fulfilling relationships, to deal with anger, to be friendly and compassionate, to have the drive to make dreams come true and pursue ambitions (self-efficacy), and to feel deeply calm.

People with early unregulated stress and nerve cell damage experience the environment more often as threatening, brood a lot, and feel an intense desire for rewards. They have difficulties in forming bonds, inhibiting their impulses, or evaluating risks. They seem rather indifferent and apathetic.

A child with an overactive stress response system is more prone to depression later in difficult life situations. Scientists are increasingly linking stress in infancy with the rapidly increasing number of anxiety disorders and depression in adolescents. Early separation from the mother also triggers an alarm reaction in the child's brain, which is similar to that of an adult suffering from clinical depression.

Not only psychological but also physical illnesses in adulthood find their cause in developmental and biological damage in the first years of life. Supposedly purely organic ailments such as diabetes, calcification of the coronary arteries, obesity, high blood pressure, and many other diseases occur more frequently. The early socio-emotional experiences are imprinted into the biological structure and show long-term effects.

Loving care in the first years of life, and the feeling of a secure bond, protect children from toxic stress. They have a safe haven where they can find comfort. They can explore their environment from this safe base. In cooperation with the sensitive bonding person, oxytocin is regularly released. Oxytocin, as a binding hormone, is an opponent of the stress hormones. In the presence of oxytocin, the stress hormones have less effect.

Margot Sunderland has written about stress regulation in her book *What Every Parent Needs to Know*. Parents who consistently calm their crying baby and take their fears seriously ensure a balanced stress regulation system. Parents become the neurochemical basis that establishes the balance of the child's emotional hormones. Children can recharge their emotional batteries with their parents. For example, children interrupt their play, then they often sit on their mother's or father's lap in the middle of a game, and after a short period of time, they continue to play. They have then been emotionally refueled. Through the brief physical contact with their confidant, they were able to establish a balance in their emotional hormones.

Up to the age of four, an infant needs emotional regulation about every twenty seconds. Obviously, this is a high need in the child and a huge task for parents.

Parents who are themselves equipped with a poorly functioning emotional regulatory system often have no understanding of their child's needs. They are not aware that their child wants to use them as a guide to get feedback on the seriousness of the situation. They are hardly able to be empathic and calm when they are faced with their baby's alarm systems.

The quality of the parent-child relationship, therefore, has a decisive influence on the ability to regulate one's own emotions and on the development of the cerebrum. Parents should take the task of being the emotional regulators for their babies very seriously. The consistent regulation of feelings by parents helps the baby to develop stress regulators.

Emotional Regulation Results in Healthy Self-Efficacy

According to Albert Bandura, emotion regulation is a factor in the development of a healthy self-efficacy. The infant is self-effective because it is able to accept failure, regulate its feelings, and not give up.

Let us take the example of self-dressing. This process usually takes four to five years for children until they can do everything themselves. Many small partial successes give courage and naturally lead to the next step. The child's intention to put on his underpants by himself needs time – a lot of time – to become a reality.

The leg is put into the wrong big hole, or suddenly two legs are stuck in one hole, and everything has to start all over again. When they have practiced enough, they will also appreciate letting mom or dad help put them on again. Later they will do another exercise session. Here children learn with trial and error. After much practice, they finally succeed. The trousers are put on, and they are in the right place. Then the child's pride is unmistakable. *I did that on my own,* they seem to express.

However, if getting dressed quickly in the morning because work calls or a doctor's appointment is due, then the child is not given the opportunity to try it out and practice. The child is dressed quickly by the parents, and then it is off to the car! In our normal daily routine, there are situations that deprive the child of the field of experience and thus also the possibility of pride in the success he has achieved himself. The daily routine and hectic pace often prevent the child from experiencing self-efficacy. Of course, such situations often cannot be avoided. It helps the child if you announce your intentions. Even babies notice it when you accompany your actions with speech.

Children who are able to regulate their feelings, and who have experienced the feeling of self-efficacy, have a much greater chance even as adults to feel self-efficacy and to act accordingly.

Self-efficacy is nowadays an important prerequisite to be successful in the labor market. Companies are desperately looking for employees with a high self-efficacy for the following reasons:

- People with high self-efficacy look for realistic and ambitious goals. They look for a match between their skills and the job requirements. People with low self-efficacy often choose goals that are too easy or too difficult (overestimation of self).

- People with high self-efficacy show greater endurance, pursue goals more persistently, increase their efforts in difficult situations, and do not give up. If they fail, they stick to their goals and will try again. They look for new and better strategies to improve their performance.

● Employees with a high level of self-efficacy increase their efforts when faced with constructive criticism from managers and colleagues. They believe that they can do it and want to prove that to others. People with low self-efficacy, on the other hand, reduce their effort in such a situation.

● Self-effective people have higher resilience in negative situations. Social conflicts, stress, and failures do not stop them, but they try to change the situations. Employees with low self-efficacy are more likely to give up or even experience a burnout.

Also, of interest for company personnel selection is that self-efficacy often correlates with relatively unchangeable personality traits such as general intelligence, conscientiousness, extroversion, and emotional stability.

Conclusion

The development of self-efficacy is highly susceptible to disruption. Parents or caregivers who react sensitively to the needs of their child are the best guarantors for the development of self-efficacy. Successful regulation of emotions and little experience of stress in infancy and toddlerhood encourage healthy psychological and physiological development. Positive experiences, imitation of role models, and encouragement of the children are equally important.

Chapter Four

My Childhood – Your Childhood

The life of the parents is the book in which
the children read.

— Augustinus Aurelius (354–430)

Family relationships are complex. Virtually everything we believe in as adults – what we pass on and what our viewpoint is – is decided by our early relationship experiences. Whether we think everything has to revolve around ourselves, whether we think we have to make a special effort to succeed, whether we think we are not worthy of attention – the list is endless.

Our parents are our first relationship. They make a significant contribution to how our first experiences are shaped. However, our parents also had parents of their own. The way they dealt with us, therefore, also depends on their first relationship with their parents. A childhood can never be viewed in isolation. It is part of a chain of childhoods of previous generations of a family. Even the quality of the grandparents' marriage can influence the views, experiences, and actions of the grandchildren.

Why we want to take up a certain profession, possibly fail at work, or have no luck in love – this and much more can be influenced by our ancestors. The most painful experiences of our ancestors, most of which have not been processed, are passed on to the following generations in so-called *soul capsules*. Such a soul capsule sometimes only opens after two or three generations. These opened soul capsules can become dramatically visible as an eating disorder, an anxiety disorder, or depression, just to name a few examples. This event then seems to come out of the blue like an unexpected and unprepared stroke of fate.

Your First Relationship Experiences

Speaking of first relationship experiences: what were your first relationship experiences?

- Did your parents react sufficiently to you, as you needed them to react?
- Did your mother enjoy being pregnant with you?
- Were you wanted, a child of love?
- Did your parents have the feeling of being loved?
- Were you allowed to be the way you are, or did you have to meet certain standards and expectations? Were you allowed to develop?
- Were you intimidated and hindered in your possibilities?
- Did you get support and encouragement? Did you have the feeling of being left alone?

Usually, parents are happy about their child and proud to be parents. The glow in the parents' eyes is a sign of their joy about their child. Every child wants to see that glow in the eyes of their parents again and again. The problem is that parents are only human beings, with their own strengths and weaknesses. The weaknesses of the parents can be the reason for dull eyes. The child will look for solutions to compensate for the weaknesses of their parents. To be able to see the shine in the eyes of their parents again, children are unconsciously willing to take everything upon themselves. The resulting shine in the parents' eyes is essential for the child's spiritual development. Only in this way can the infant experience itself as someone positive and valuable.

Why We Create Loyalty Contracts

To achieve this shine in the eyes of the parents, every child, without exception, enters into a tacit *loyalty contract* with its parents and will fulfil it unconditionally.

Sabine Lück and Ingrid Alexander, psychological psychotherapists, child and youth psychotherapists, developed the generation code to heal hereditary wounds.

What is such a contract of loyalty about; what is the content of such a contract?

Nobody had really well-fitting parents as a child — those parents who would have provided us with the care we needed. Parents also carry with them their own childhood deficits, which interfere with the parents' lives and which do not let them react in the way that would be appropriate for the child.

A deficit, for example, could be when a mother who did not feel loved as a child now expects her child to give this love. A father who has never been able to fulfil his dream job now expects his child to do this job. He projects his own unfulfilled dreams into future fantasies and expectations for his child.

A mother confuses her own neediness with love, and so she will only turn lovingly to the child if this child satisfies her needs and fulfils her expectations. *Be as I want you and I need you to be.* The child will learn that it is to blame if the mother is dissatisfied or unhappy. The child will try unsuccessfully to get her love, always hoping to get her love eventually.

Parents who need their children to compensate for parental deficits are described in great detail and vividly by Dr. Maaz in his book *The False Self.*

How should parents deal with their deficits? What are their options? The answer is very simple: if parents knew the far-reaching effects their behaviour patterns have on their children, they would work on these patterns and change them.

Most parents do not know the causes and effects of their deficits. On the contrary, they avoid them in order to avoid having to relive the old, strong feelings of their own childhood. Thus, everything continues along the familiar paths and often results in a dead end.

From the child's point of view, children want to strengthen and heal their parents. Subconsciously, they believe that they know the way out of the dead end. Children intuitively know what their parents are missing in order to be suitable parents. Children believe that they can heal their parents if they give the part of themselves to the parents that the parents are missing. As a consequence, the child can no longer experience this part of its own personality. Children are willing to pay this price so that in their imagination, the parents are then perfectly fitting — as perfectly fitting as the child needs them to be. These would be ideal parents who could finally give the child what it needs to develop a stable ego.

Therefore, every child enters into a loyalty contract with its parents. Figuratively speaking, we each sign a separate loyalty contract with our father and another with our mother. The recognized deficit of the parents will be compensated with a gift from the child, thus protecting the deficient parent. The following example will help to demonstrate.

Anna's Loyalty Contract

A mother — let's call her Anna — sits by the side of a pool in the summer. Her boys are high-spirited, full of zest for life, and romp around in the water. Her daughter Lena sits next to her but is reluctant to participate. She is the smallest, youngest of the children. Anna is asked by her boys to take part in this wonderful spectacle of the joy of life. She enjoys watching her group of children, but she also realizes that it is impossible for her to take part in this excitement. Something prevents her from taking part in this display of zest for life. She remains sitting at the edge of the pool, with the feeling that something is missing.

Coming to terms with this situation brings astonishing things to light. Anna, for her part, had a mother (Emma) who lacked a zest for life. In order to get a suitable mother, to see the shine in Emma's eyes, Anna had already given her own zest for life to her mother in early childhood. Here the unspoken, subconscious loyalty contract of the child (Anna) to the mother (Emma) is called, *Never in my life will I feel more zest for life than you (mother) could and can ever feel it.*

If the child would enjoy great joy of life, then the mother would become aware again of this sore point in her life. It would be painful for Emma and hurt her if she saw what she could have experienced as a child with a permitted joy of life. Emma would have to acknowledge how much happier she would have been if she had been given permission to enjoy life. Emma needs permission to be fun-loving, not from her child, but from her own parents. Emma cannot even perceive the gift from her child Anna, let alone accept it. The child's given joy of life is, therefore, of no use to either the mother or the child. The *joie de vivre* of both mother and daughter hovers unused in the room.

In other words, because of the mother's inability to feel joy for life, she cannot give her child the permission to enjoy life. The child — existentially dependent — fulfils the mother's wish. The child, thus, protects the mother, and the mother is not confronted with her pain. A loyalty contract can, therefore, block the development of our own personality. As a child, we sacrifice important parts of ourselves for our parents to help them become the parents we so desperately need. As a result, we cannot build up partial aspects of our own identity.

Now comes the dilemma. This loyalty contract, which is individually concluded by each of us, binds us for our whole life.

In our lives, we subconsciously look for people and situations that confirm the correctness of our loyalty contract. In our example, it is safer for Anna not to feel any joy for life. She avoids corresponding situations (taking part in the excitement in the swimming pool), or she looks for people in her life who kill the fun.

Children are highly loyal to their parents. This loyalty can go so far that we look for partners whose characteristics and deficits are very similar to our respective parent. These characteristics and deficits feel very familiar to us. Unfortunately, we sometimes confuse this familiarity, the sense of *feeling at home*, with love.

For another reason, we are always looking for people who are similar to our parents in terms of our loyalty contract. We had to experience that our gift was not accepted. Also, it is not possible to take back a gift. Therefore, we hope to find someone who will finally accept our gift of joy for life, but this will never happen.

The chain of relationship experiences or loyalty contracts can be passed on from generation to generation. In our example, Lena (Anna's daughter) also sits at the edge of the pool instead of playing wildly with her brothers. Superficially, there is an obvious reason: she is a girl among all the boys, she is the youngest, the smallest. It is forgotten that she is very experienced in dealing with her older brothers and that the superficial attempt at an explanation is without substance.

Rather, the entire family system would have to be considered in this situation. Is it possible that Anna (Lena's mother) is the reason for Lena's behaviour? Lena has a loyalty contract with her mother and protects her by sitting at the edge of the pool. All this happens subconsciously.

Such situations have to be questioned to bring about a change for the better.

Loyalty Contracts and Asking Key Questions

Loyalty contracts can be terminated. In order to cancel a loyalty contract, you must first know the contract.

You must approach the content of your own loyalty contract with key questions. You ask *yourself* these key questions, not your parents.

You must be aware that we have concluded two loyalty contracts, one with the mother and one with the father. One contract is with the same-sex parent: the daughter with the mother or the son with the father. The other contract is with the opposite-sex parent: from son to mother or from daughter to father. The key question to ask the same-sex parent is:

What am I not allowed to outdo my mother/father in?

In our example, Anna was not allowed to outdo her mother, Emma, on the subject of joy for life, never feeling more joy for life than her mother. The key question to ask the opposite sex parent is different. The key question from the daughter to the father is:

What am I not allowed to do in order not to disappoint my father?

The son has to answer the question:

What can I not abandon my mother for?

Paul's Loyalty Contract

Paul is very successful in his professional life. He is socially very competent, very empathetic, but you notice that he has always lived alone. He spends his vacations with his mother, who has also always lived alone. You have never experienced him in a partnership. Physical closeness during a hug or greeting seems to be unpleasant for him.

Let us ask Paul the key question: *What can he not abandon his mother for?*

He could give the following answer: "I can't abandon my mother. No one must be closer to me than my mother. I must not find anyone in my life who is more important to me than my mother. I'll never meet anyone who cares for me the way my mother does."

Paul's loyalty contract has become visible. It defines his whole life. Could you imagine a partner who would accept this loyalty contract? It is not surprising that Paul remains alone as long as he does not terminate his contract.

How to Terminate Loyalty Contracts

The cancellation of the loyalty contract feels like a betrayal of the parents. You must have the courage to summon up the will to embark on something new and unknown. But keep in mind that this does not mean that you throw away the skills you acquired by fulfilling the contract. Now you will use these skills for yourself, instead of using them to protect your parents.

Another essential prerequisite for a successful termination is to stop believing that you can make up for, or are responsible for, your parents' deficits, or that you can save your parents from their pain.

Imagine the respective parent without deficit and without old wounds. Without these deficits and wounds, we now have parents who fit perfectly and who adequately meet our needs. We can now experience the fulfillment of our needs and save the imagined positive feelings we have experienced as a memory.

This new emotional memory overwrites the old loyalty contract. We have created a new "old" reality for ourselves — a *remembered present*. This is possible because the same brain structures are active when we remember the past and when we develop imaginary scenes in the present.

In daily life, we can imagine a mother who provides us with the right care in the situation at hand, a mother who is the way we would have needed her. We should imagine and feel in detail how well she provides for us and what she advises us.

From our example, Anna would visualize a mother as she would have needed her. This perfectly fitting mother would have played with her and would have had joy with her. She would have raved with her, laughed, and jumped into the pool with her.

Anna would think, *If I had had a mother as I needed her, she would have walked with me laughing through a flowery meadow in summer, and in the end, she would have let herself fall with me into the splendor of the flowers.*

These fantasies can be difficult at first because they are so unusual. But I promise it gets easier every time you visualize. You may even have thoughts that you never thought possible.

It is important to know that parents without deficits do not exist. We cannot prevent loyalty contracts because they are vital for our survival as infants. But we have to realize that these loyalty contracts have become obsolete in our adult lives.

In the present, they only hinder us without us realizing it. We must consciously question them. The loyalty contracts, which were made at an age when our consciousness was not yet sufficiently developed, have a life-determining effect. Only when we are aware that we would have needed other parents for our own healthy development do the loyalty contracts lose their power.

A dissolved loyalty contract will have a positive effect on all our habits. It is like removing the foundation of our paradigms. To be truly authentic, we must learn to distinguish which of our actions correspond to our own life goals, and which of them we have adopted to heal our family system.

Past Feelings Influence Us Today

Memories of our old feelings, and the reawakening of associated memories, influence our dealings with others — especially with our children. Children always manage to trigger these old feelings in us. They have the best access to them because we are emotionally and deeply connected to them. Without being aware of it, we do not react appropriately in the here and now, but to the reactivated feelings from our own childhood in the past.

It is important to learn to distinguish the old feelings of the past from the appropriate feelings of today. Feelings that we perceive when we are with our children can sometimes take our breath away or knock us off our feet. If we are inundated with feelings, reflected thinking is hardly possible. These feelings are most likely childhood memories — strong feelings that cause us to react as a child would rather than as an adult.

Imagine that a daughter comes home from school, throws her backpack in the corner, and screams: "That stupid Nina, she's not my girlfriend anymore!"

You can sense that you have plenty of advice to help her in this situation of her supposed disappointment, but beware: you may be the one feeling disappointment, and at the same time, have a feeling of anger. But your daughter may not have that same feeling of anger. Your own anger originates in the experiences of your own childhood; you should make sure whether your daughter is really angry. You may have forgotten to check this reality, as opposed to reacting from the experiences of your own childhood.

The advice you are now conjuring up for your child is from your own memories. Whether or not it would really help her is debatable, nor do you consider if the advice really would have helped you back then. You are not in the here and now. You are still trapped in the memory of your old emotional experiences in your past.

Is your daughter only disappointed about the behaviour of her friend, or is she actually angry as well?

Take a deep breath and have a reality check before speaking. For instance, ask your daughter, "What is going to happen with you and Nina now?"

Imagine your amazement when you hear her answer: "Oh, she will definitely call later and want to play with me again!"

So, you have confused your own childhood with your daughter's, and at the same time, you have been triggered at your sore spot of how you deal with anger and disappointment. Your old feelings from your childhood have come back to you.

You would have been immediately ready with all kinds of advice, which may not have actually helped you at that time in your childhood. And you would have passed on your own problem of dealing with disappointment and anger to your daughter unchecked. These old feelings belong in the past and have no place in the here and now with your daughter.

This example was quite obvious. Children enjoy poking around in our hidden, masked views that are based on our own early experiences.

For another example, during the school enrolment examination, parents often report their great concern about whether their fidgety child will be able to cope with school. Surely their child has to sit quietly in the classroom to follow the lessons.

When asked who in the family their child takes after, the parents usually spontaneously think of someone, such as an uncle. Further inquiries make it clear that this uncle is successful. Now it usually comes out that the parent's brother (the child's uncle) used to get on the family's nerves terribly, like their child. He always was on the move. He never really rested, and his attention would constantly change direction, from one idea to another.

This comparison sets the parents at ease since they can relate their child's behaviour to that of a successful relative. In addition, they have an expert fidgeter in the family that they can turn to for advice when they run into an issue with their child. Based on his own experience, the uncle is the best person to explain what is behind the child's behaviour. He is also a family expert, due to his own childhood, in the question of what support his nephew could best receive at the moment.

Subconscious Double Messages

Children can also uncover our double messages. In a normal human interaction, meaning is delivered only a little with words, but mostly with emotional expression and tone and with body language. In a double message, we speak or act differently than we think or feel. The *acting* corresponds to the verbal level. The *thinking and feeling* correspond to the emotional level.

If your child constantly displays behaviour that annoys you, and no matter what you do, it does not change. You even have the impression that it is getting worse. This is a sign that the behaviour has something to do with you and your own childhood. For some reason, you subconsciously support this annoying behaviour of your child. It could be a blind spot, something that you have repressed because it makes you uncomfortable.

It is important for you to find out exactly what this has to do with you and what you can change about yourself because only then will you have a positive influence on the annoying behaviour of your child.

For example, a preteen son causes problems for his parents because he attracts attention at school with inappropriate behaviour. He irritates the teachers to the point of rage, and nothing is more important to him than to get into conflict and be unbending, no matter what the cost. His performance at school declines.

Under the pressure of his declining academic performance, the investigation revealed the following: the father himself had been expelled from school at this age because he preferred to play soccer instead of taking care of his performance at school. To this day, the father had not forgiven his teachers for not supporting and motivating him. He could only start his professional career after going back to school later and graduating.

His outward reactions to his son's behaviour were that he scolded him and punished him when he messed up again at school. But inwardly, the father was pleased that his son had the courage and daring to let the teachers run aground like that.

This behaviour is a typical subconscious double message. The son perceived this inner joy of the father at his own wrongdoing and reacted accordingly motivated. Once the father recognized these connections and stopped sending double messages, the son ended the conflicts with his teachers. He no longer had to *do something* on behalf of his father.

Conclusion

Experiences in relationships — both positive and negative — are inherited over generations. Without exception, every child establishes a *loyalty contract* with its parents. This loyalty contract can lead to unwanted behavioural and emotional blockages later in life. We should know the contents of our loyalty contracts and terminate them.

Chapter Five

———◦◆◦———

How Bonding is Created

With a childhood full of love, however, you can spend
half a life in the cold world.

—Jean Paul (1763–1825)

Attachment is the attraction between people, the striving for familiarity and closeness. We are bonding beings, whether we are aware of it or not. For children, attachment to an adult is even an absolute necessity of life.

In the 1950s, U.S. psychologist Harry Harlow conducted a series of experiments with rhesus monkeys. He separated the monkeys from their mothers immediately after birth. As a substitute, they were given a milk-donating *wire nut* — a wire frame with a milk bottle — and a *towel nut* — a wire frame covered with terry cloth, which also had a face-like head.

Harlow observed the behaviour of the rhesus monkeys and noticed that they stayed almost exclusively with the *towel nut* and only changed to the *wire nut* for drinking. With this experiment, he proved that pure physical contact is at least as important, if not more important, than physical nutrition for rhesus monkey babies.

There is a four-minute video on YouTube that shows notable scenes of this experiment. Enter "Harlow's Monkeys" as a search term and then select "The Sasss1" video.

Behavioral biologists refer to human children as carrying a *bonding instinct*. The willingness of the infant to bond with a parent is biologically anchored and gives the child security and protection. The parents' caring behaviour, their willingness to ensure the safety and protection of their child, develops in a suitable manner as early as during pregnancy.

At least two people are required for a bond. The emotional bond of a toddler to its parents is extremely important for the child's further development. A positive emotional bond is a prerequisite for the survival of a baby as well as for building trust and bonds with other people.

Basic Physical and Emotional Needs

Basic physical needs, such as food, drink, sleep, or warmth, must be met. Everyone understands this and knows that we will die without enough food or drink. The same applies to the need for sleep and warmth. The non-fulfilment of basic physical needs leads to death. The reaction to a lack of physical needs is experienced promptly.

Basic emotional needs have the same significance. These are the needs for security and orientation, belonging and bonding, appreciation and self-esteem, as well as curiosity and joy. A lack of satisfying basic emotional needs can lead to various diseases and can also lead to death. Examples of diseases that such a lack can lead to are mental illnesses such as depression, anorexia, and addiction disorders.

The reaction to a lack of satisfaction with basic emotional needs can be delayed far into adult life, sometimes even fifty or sixty years. It could be that this is the reason why the absolute necessity to satisfy mental needs is not well known. It can take humans so long to see results that we often do not make a connection between childhood experiences and later problems or disease.

Let us take a closer look at the basic needs of the soul. There are different descriptions, and their meanings are evaluated differently. However, there is no universally valid definition of basic emotional needs.

According to Albert Pesso, the United States pioneer of body psychotherapy, the vital needs are for space, food, support, hold (bonding), protection, and boundaries.

According to the German psychologist and communication scientist Friedemann Schulz von Thun, the following four needs are in the foreground of emotional needs:

- To be valuable
- To be loved
- To be free
- To be attached

The need for attachment is a core need. How does bonding develop, which is so important for our healthy emotional growth?

The way in which parents respond to their child's signals and needs is very important and decisive in the formation of a bond. Depending on how well parents respond to their baby's basic needs, babies develop a better or worse bond with the person who cares for them. In the beginning, the bonding person is usually the mother. If this relationship provides sufficient security, protection, and love, a secure bond is formed. If the baby experiences a reliable response to their signals every day, then they feel safe. Due to parental sensitivity, safely bonded children develop great confidence with the person who is responsible for the bond. The child feels that its feelings and needs are in order and experiences the world as a safe place. Basic trust develops, and with it, the basis for a healthy emotional self-image.

Children who have experienced rejection — or who have had the experience that their signals were not recognized, not answered appropriately, or even answered wrongly — do not develop a secure bond. They cannot come to the conclusion that they are entitled to love and support and bury their desires deep within themselves. A harmful interpersonal environment – for instance, unreliable or changing reactions to the baby's signals, or neglect and traumatic experiences — prevent a secure bond.

The Bonding Theory

John Bowlby, a British pediatrician and psychotherapist, and Mary Ainsworth, a Canadian psychologist, were the ones who researched bonding and developed the bonding theory. If you want to understand this theory in more detail, watch an easy-to-understand cartoon video on YouTube. Enter "The Attachment Theory" as a search term and select the "Sprouts" video.

The bonding style we develop as a baby remains with us for a lifetime. It determines how we feel, whether the glass is half full or half empty, and whether we *dare* or give up quickly.

A stable psyche with a stable sense of "I" needs stable bonding. Prof. Klaus Grawe, psychologist (1943—2005), describes the insecure attachments acquired in childhood as the greatest known risk factors for the development of mental disorders occurring in later life.

Very helpful for further understanding is the description of the Canadian psychologist Gordon Neufeld about the development of attachment in six stages, each one deeper and later than the other.

In the *first stage*, the bond is created through the senses with the aim of experiencing physical closeness. The baby perceives its attachment person sensually. It wants to be able to touch, hear, see, and smell them; this stage is the bonding stage.

In the *second stage* of developing attachment, the child wants to be like his closest caregivers and, through imitation and emulation, adopts their manners and expressions. The bond is created through togetherness and common interests. For example, the acquisition of language happens through imitation. Neufeld speaks of the stage of equality; *me too* is the motto of this phase.

The *third stage* is when loyalty and belonging are in the foreground. In this phase, being close to a person means considering them as one's own. Everyone knows the claims of ownership that children at this age make to their attachment figures: my mommy, my daddy!

The *fourth stage*, striving for closeness and connection, is the search for meaning, the feeling of being important to someone. Children live for the happy expressions of their parents. The problem with this phase of attachment is the child's great vulnerability; they suffer when they feel that they are not important to their attachment person.

During the *fifth stage*, the child itself perceives feelings of affection, love, care, and warmth for the other. For example, children often fall in love with their attachment figure. The children give their heart as a gift.

The last and *sixth stage* of bonding is familiarity. To trust someone is to feel close to them. If a child seeks closeness in this way, they will share their secrets. The child whispers its secrets in the ear of their caregiver, usually the parents. There is no greater closeness than the feeling of being able to trust someone, to be liked and accepted for who and what you are.

Given the central importance of attachment for the child's development and psyche, the person with whom the child has the most intense attachment will always be the person with the greatest importance for the child. In fact, the mother usually plays the main role in the attachment. This seems to be biologically based.

The Mother-Child Relationship

The psychiatrist and depth psychologist Hans-Joachim Maaz describes the special nature of the mother-child relationship as follows:

> "It should be noted that the earliest relationships during pregnancy, birth, and lactation give the natural mother a privileged relationship meaning for the child, from which other caregivers (father, grandmother, childminder, daycare educator) remain excluded. This special rank of a mother is only gradually realized in the development of the child and should never be given up or questioned too early or too abruptly. The child unconsciously experiences feelings of inferiority, self-esteem doubts and self-insecurity when separated too early."

> "According to all that we know today in terms of developmental psychology," writes Maaz, "the real

mother with her maternity remains the most important reference person for the child for about three years."

In this context, Maaz *maternally* understands the ability and willingness to listen, to empathize, to confirm, to protect, and to care. The maternal figure is responsible for the development of the bond, self-esteem, and identity of the later adult. This means that too early a separation leads to a total lack of experience of maternal love that cannot be replaced by anyone else.

Answer for yourself the following questions about your childhood experiences:

- Am I wanted?
- Am I loved? (for my own sake or only if I meet expectations?)
- Am I allowed to be the way I am? (according to my possibilities and limitations) Or do I have to meet expectations and standards?

These questions concern the experiences that arise from the quality of motherhood.

The Father-Child Relationship

Of course, fathers should not be missing. Children need fathers and fathering. With the help of the fathers, the exciting world can be explored. The following questions concern the quality of fathering:

- Am I allowed to develop? (Or am I intimidated and hindered?)

- Do I receive beneficial guidance, support, encouragement? (Or am I left alone?)
- Is my limitation accepted?

Being fatherly means having the ability and willingness to accompany, support, encourage, and challenge. Fatherliness supports and develops autonomy, achievement, sense of duty, responsibility, and world-shaping.

Parental Deficits

What problems parents have with motherhood or fatherhood, again, depend on what experiences they had in their own childhood. Parents who themselves experienced too little motherly or fatherly love find it difficult to love children. They want to be loved by their children as compensation. They cannot feel what is right or wrong and will rely on the advice of counselors and act accordingly. Parents who have experienced too little fatherly love often demand more from the child than they are capable of.

A mother who experienced too little motherly love even as a child could compensate by loving her child above all to protect the child from the lack she herself experienced. Whether this "love of happiness" or "too much love" is the right thing for the child is left to be decided.

Self-experienced deficits are subconsciously passed on by the parents to their children. Self-awareness and reflection help us emotionally to process the consequences of self-inflicted injuries and deficits. Through the knowledge of the deficits, we succeed in not letting ourselves be defined or deterred by them, in not giving them any more power over our actions. With this knowledge, we achieve a better quality of life for ourselves as well as for our children.

Conclusion

The baby is born unfinished. A successful attachment to its first caregiver, naturally the mother, is the basis for the child to develop a healthy, strong personality for life. A secure bond in childhood promotes the establishment of fulfilling relationships in adulthood. Conversely, unsuccessful bonding experiences can lead to severe psychological and social disorders in adulthood.

Chapter Six

Quality Needs Quantity

It's really clear that the most precious resource we all have is time.

— Steve Jobs (1955—2011)

Quality *before quantity* has become a familiar term these days. In almost all areas of life, the call for quality is getting louder and louder. Even in the leisure sector, there is a quality offensive. Parents are also advised to spend *quality time* with their children.

What Is Quality Time?

But what does *quality* actually mean? There is no uniform definition of quality. Possible definitions are that quality is the expression of meeting expectations or the degree of correspondence between the demands of a product and its properties. One could also say that quality is what the customer wants. Companies have even specialized in finding out what customers want. Based on this knowledge, a product is developed that meets the customer's expectations a little more than the competitor's product. With this quality approach, a lot of money can be earned. A customer is satisfied with the quality of a product if it meets his expectations. Why are such considerations in this book? Here the focus is on ourselves, our relationships, our childhood, and our children. In private life, we like to use the term *quality time*. This term suggests something positive as if we were experiencing something with quality. Yet quality time has very little in common with quality.

The term was invented by adults to try to ease their guilty consciences, the guilty conscience that stirs when it becomes clear that there is too little time in the daily routine. This applies both to partner relationships and parent-child relationships. If we already have too little time just to be with each other, then at least let us spend the remaining time together intensively. This concept of quality is expected to absolve us of the feelings of guilt.

Imagine you are newly in love. You have met a great person and are floating on cloud nine. What is your most fervent wish? What both of you want most of all is to spend the whole day together, every hour, every minute. The whole reality consists only of time together. Any separation from the beloved is hardly bearable. Everyone knows that. Fortunately, we have a mind that helps us.

After this first intense phase is going well, then we slowly start to perceive the world and the reality around us again. We listen again to our circle of friends, which we might have neglected a little. We also bear it well when our partner temporarily goes off on his own. In the meantime, we have built up so much trust in each other that we can rely on each other. Because of the relationship, we trust each other that we will get together again. Each one of us relies on the other one to do his best to contribute to the success of the relationship. We have given away our hearts.

What would it mean for you if your partner suddenly came up with the proposal to limit your relationship to *quality time* from now on? Quality time would then be full of activities on the weekend.

Since the rest of the time is otherwise scarce for your partner, he would be replaced by someone else from Monday to Wednesday from now on, and on Thursday and Friday, he would fortunately also find a replacement for you.

That does not sound so good for you anymore. But this is exactly what many children have experienced in the past. And nowadays, many small children are expected to do so, as replacements such as educators, childminders, and nannies are caregivers. Infants who spend the whole day in a group, away from the people they fell in love with, have a lack of care. Parents often try to make the remaining, scarce time as meaningful as possible after their working hours and on weekends. Despite well-meant intentions, they insist there will be quality time, even when they do not feel like it at all. Children notice this intuitively. For them, this is no longer quality time, because their expectations of unconditional time together are not fulfilled.

What Is Quantity Time?

In many parenting guides, the tip for the first year of life is *Spend as much time with your child as possible!* That sounds like *quantity* time. Quality, from the child's point of view, is the desire for time together. This expectation is not limited to the first year of life.

In all the countless million-dollar guidebooks for troubled partner relationships, you will always find the tip to spend more unplanned time with your partner. You should always show (not just tell) your partner that the relationship with him or her is important to you. Obviously, we measure our importance to another person also by the time that other person spends with us. Children could also measure their importance in this way. According to surveys, the number one relationship killer is lack of time. Parents are even advised to allow themselves more time as a couple without the children.

To build and maintain a relationship, people need a lot of time with each other — this is called *quantity*. This time spent together then fulfils the expectations of the other — this is called *quality*. In short, without quantity, there is no quality.

In this context, the other expectations of children towards their parents can be summarized simply: time, attention, and tenderness.

So, it is time to rethink the term *quality time* and fill it with new content. If parents want to spend quality time with their children, everyone should understand that the parents want to spend *enough time* with their children. The relationship should not be timed or adapted to the parents' schedule. A limited period of time (such as one hour) of intensive attention is not enough to build a sustainable relationship between parents and children in the long run.

For example, the ten-year-old daughter of a client (a mother) has made this quite clear to her mother. The mother had little time for her for months because she was very busy at work. During the family vacation, the mother wanted to make up for everything. She had planned to romp with her daughter in the waves for at least an hour every day. After presenting her offer of time to her daughter, she received an unexpected answer: "I don't have time to go into the water with you now. Do you think just because you have time now, I feel like it?"

Conclusion

Quantity in the parent-child relationship means to spend as much unconditional and unplanned time together as possible. We should consider whether we should not simply delete the term *quality time* from our vocabulary.

Chapter Seven

What Parents and Children Really Need

There are no great discoveries and advances, as long as there is an unhappy child on earth.

— Albert Einstein (1879—1955)

After you have read this book, you will know the answers to the question posed by this chapter's title. It is a serious task to nurture children as they grow up.

Following your own intuition is not enough. Your own intuition is based (how could it be otherwise?) on your own imperfect childhood. We have taken in a lot of subconscious orders, messages, and scripts from our family and our ancestors, and we have passed them on to our children without reflection. We cannot simply get out of the past. Even the decision to try to provide the opposite of what we have experienced is just another form of adaptation and not a real exit. We have not made a real new decision; we have just chosen the opposite out of simple resistance.

What Parents Need to Know

Parents need sufficient information about the mental and physical developmental steps of a child, and what support the child needs for each next developmental step.

Parents need a willingness to think about themselves. They should get to know their own childhood again. Only then can the reasons for their own actions in their role as father or mother be explored. Once I have become clear about my own childhood, I have to ask myself whether I want to pass on my own experiences and actions, which I have made conscious, to my children.

Possibly, the answer to your question will initiate a change. Such changes are an opportunity to interrupt unwanted behaviour and to develop personality in your child.

Your Social Network's Reaction

A person's social network and friends will react to these changes. This opens perhaps a critical dialogue. Everyone in the circle might call their own assumptions and experiences into question, and they may want to defend themselves from any new realizations. The parents will need stability to present their own development to the social environment.

Let us assume that a young, successful woman would like to be just a mother for a while. She has come to this decision after honest and careful self-reflection. Her social environment will question this decision and provoke reactions.

Possibly her mother will react critically because this decision would put her daughter in a financial dependency. Maybe friends cannot understand the possible interruption of her career and warn her of the prospect of becoming an *unsatisfied mother hen.* Society will not adequately reward her efforts as a mother only.

The young woman should contrast these objections with her own knowledge and needs and weigh them up honestly. Why does she want to be a mother? *The young woman should know that a mother is the most important relationship person for her child.* Through pregnancy, birth, and breastfeeding, maternal influence dominates with formative experiences for the whole life of the child. With good motherhood, a child feels welcomed and wanted, and its needs are met; it is cared for, protected, and comforted. Thus, the foundation is laid for the development of a secure and self-effective person who can fully develop to their personal potential.

The Father's Important Role

Although the father can neither give birth nor nurse, he has a no less important task to nurture the child's development. The father gradually softens the close relationship between mother and child. He is the person who supports the child, helping it to risk the distance from the mother in order to explore the world joyfully. The father embodies the detachment, the autonomy, the adventure, the new, and the foreign. With good paternity, the child experiences interest in its possibilities and understanding of its difficulties.

In another scenario, a man has been a devoted and empathetic father to his son until his twelfth birthday. Suddenly the father/child relationship gets a crack in it. Subconsciously, the father suddenly turns away from his child and is hardly available for joint activities. At first, neither of them understands what is happening. Although the father wants something different, he cannot get out of his skin at first.

After coming to terms with his own childhood, it becomes clear to the father that he cannot fall back on any of the experiences that a father has with his child at that age. He lost his own father when he was twelve years old. By imagining what he would have needed, he can now develop his own ideas, a plan, and thus actively change his behaviour towards the child.

Reality Check and Small Steps

I hope you have taken some suggestions with you that will motivate you to take a closer look. If you are overwhelmed by your emotions, you can do a reality check. You can also use your imagination to create an image of your suitable parents. Maybe this will make you more self-confident, more courageous, and more willing to take the risk of changing. *The fear of change comes from your childhood and has no place in the here and now.*

Do you not know where to begin? You can start with small, concrete steps. Why not go through your habits. Habits are reflex-like ways of acting and reacting.

Make a list of habits in your life that you would like to change. Write down your *bad* habits that annoy you and that you want to change. For example: Why can't you wait? Why do you say so often *I can't do that!*? Why do you have to check everything?

After a personal evaluation, sort the list according to importance. Start with your number one habit and consider what and how you want to change.

All of your listed bad habits cannot be changed at once! No habit can be changed in passing, in a hurry. Be patient with yourself!

Pay Attention to Your Language

Pay attention to your language. If possible, use only positive statements and no negations when talking to small children. The word *not* is often used when talking to children. But children cannot hear this small but important word. If you say, *Don't fidget around like that,* the toddler will understand only *fidget around.* Instead, use a positive invitation in your speech, such as *Stay seated,* while offering something interesting in addition. The word *don't* should not be used in infancy.

Try to express your concern; for instance, try to adapt the reflexive exclamation *Watch out— don't fall off the climbing frame* to avoid using the word *don't*; replace it with a positive statement!

A four-year-old boy full of discovery had climbed onto a ten-meter-high spruce tree. When the mother noticed this, she wanted to shout in the first reflex: *Be careful! Do not fall down!* She succeeded in suppressing her impulse of fear. Instead, she expressed happiness with him and offered him an ice cream so that he had a reason to climb down. She trusted his abilities and left him unattended, then prepared the promised ice cream rather than standing next to the tree full of worry and possibly unsettling him with her fear. After this story came to a good end, the following night, the mother took a saw and removed all branches within her reach.

Recognize Connections

Another example is of a young mother who asked me for medicine to strengthen her unhappy five-year-old son. In the course of further conversation, the supposed weakness of the son crystallized — the son reacted unhappily to his really annoying cousin. His mother had already recognized this, but she did not dare to interrupt the play meetings. She feared that her younger sister (the mother of the annoying cousin) would not understand this temporary interruption. As a child, she had often been responsible for the welfare of her younger sister. Once she realized these connections, she took heart, acted to protect her son, and learned to say *No* to her sister.

This *No* meant, for her, no more responsibility for her sister's welfare, no more forcing the son to play with the annoying cousin, and no need for medication for her son.

Roots in Early Childhood

The experiences in the first years of life are decisive for the entire later life of every human being. How an adult behaves in their professional and private life, which health strengths or problems they develop, whether they become a hypochondriac or a person without health concerns, whether they act confidently or anxiously — all these things have their roots in early childhood.

Did you receive enough attention and tenderness? A deficit in attention is the beginning of a constant search for balance throughout your later life. The choice of and interaction with a person's life partner, friends, and surroundings are shaped by this deficit and the search for compensation. The woman or man with a deficit in attention from parents at a young age could develop narcissistic or perfectionist traits. In professional life, these people may be very successful. Their hunger for attention drives their willingness to perform; but success does not make these people happy, and it does not satisfy them. Success cannot compensate for the deficits experienced. They have to go on and on, remaining empty inside. It was not success they were looking for; it was the parental attention they had wanted in childhood. In the long term, such an unfulfilled need can lead to addictive behaviour, depression, and burnout, and also to physical suffering. The ability to believe in oneself and in one's ability to cope with something is laid as a basis in early attachment.

Unfortunately, it is becoming more and more problematic, socially, to take the time for children who really need it. In recent years, families feel as though they have been relieved of their responsibilities because children spend less time with their families and have been in all-day institutions that claim to have the child's best interest at heart. The opposite is actually the best for children.

Animal Kingdom and Bonding

We are very sensitive to animals in the area of bonding. Perhaps this is due to the relatively short period of time in which the consequences of harmful influences become visible in animals. In humans, the interval between adverse influences and the effects is sometimes fifty years or more. This blurs the connection between cause and effect. In bitches and puppies, it is considered an advantage if they are allowed to stay together for a long time. In Germany, the legal minimum time is eight weeks. It is proven that the early separation of the puppy from its mother and siblings is traumatic. Puppies who are separated from their mother too early are often later insecure, anxious, or even neurotic.

In the 1990s, in South Africa's Pilanesberg National Park, it was observed that young elephants attacked and killed a total of almost forty young rhinoceros bulls. The same thing happened a little later in another South African wildlife park. The special and unusual aspect was that the elephants actively and brutally attacked the rhinos. Behavioral researchers finally found an explanation.

The young bull elephants had been relocated from another park as orphans and had received no parental care. They also lacked the reprimands of the older elephants. However, the killings stopped when adult bull elephants were brought into the park. Under their influence, the young ones' behaviour patterns returned to normal.

Farmers have started to separate cows and calves later than they used to. They want to allow cows and calves a longer bonding time together. Positive, motivating effects are evident. Calves that grow up in a close and long relationship with their mother are healthier as adult animals; they have fewer infections and behavioural problems. The bottom line is that the farmers have significantly lowered costs for conventional husbandry by keeping cows and calves together longer.

Conclusion

Childhood determines your life. Different theories describe and explain childhood with different vocabularies, but they all draw the same conclusion:

Our behaviour begins and is founded in our childhood.

Recommended Books

Maria Steuer personally recommends these books to help further your knowledge about the topics in each of the chapters.

Chapter Two: Why Not Just Do It Differently?

Eric Berne, M.D. — *Games People Play*

Chapter Three: You Can't Change Anything Anyway

Margot Sunderland – *What Every Parent Needs to Know*

Nicole Strüber – *Risiko Kindheit*

Chapter Four: My Childhood — Your Childhood

Hans-Joachim Maaz – *Das falsche Selbst*
Sabine Lück / Ingrid Alexander – *Ahnen auf die Couch*

Chapter Five: How Bonding Is Created

Gordon Neufeld — *Hold On to Your Kids*

Chapter Six: Quality Needs Quantity

Deborah MacNamara – *Rest Play Grow*

About the Author

Maria Steuer is a renowned pediatrician and family therapist based in Germany. She specializes in examining the root cause of childhood behavioral patterns. As a doctor for Germany's education system, she has advised more than 20,000 parents on childhood behavior issues. Maria is also a mother who has experienced the ups and downs of raising her own three children. Her mission today is to help parents around the world realize how their own childhood experiences influence their habits, expectations, and belief systems. She also helps parents understand how they unconsciously transmit these habits, expectations, and beliefs to their children.

Giving a Voice to Creativity!

With every donation, a voice will be given to
the creativity that lies within the hearts of
our children living with diverse challenges.

By making this difference, children that may
not have been given the opportunity to have their
Heart Heard will have the freedom to create
beautiful works of art and musical creations.

Donate by visiting

HeartstobeHeard.com

We thank you.

Made in the USA
Coppell, TX
25 April 2021